Bhimrao Ambedkar
The Boy Who Asked Why

Bhimrao Ambedkar: The Boy Who Asked Why (English)

ISBN 978-0-9995476-1-8
© *text* Sowmya Rajendran
© *illustrations* Satwik Gade

First published in the United States in 2018 by
KitaabWorld, LLC
PO Box 268, Menlo Park, CA 94026
www.KitaabWorld.com
For information about special discounts for bulk purchases, please email contact@kitaabworld.com

First published in India in 2015 by
Tulika Publishers
24/1 Ganapathy Colony Third Street, Teynampet, Chennai 600 018, India
email reachus@tulikabooks.com *website* www.tulikabooks.com

No part of this publication may be reproduced, stored in a retrieval system or transmitted, in any format or by any means — electronic, mechanical, photocopying, recording or otherwise — without prior written permission from the publisher, except for the inclusions of brief quotations in a review.

Library of Congress Control Number: 2017958905

Printed in the United States of America

Bhimrao Ambedkar
THE BOY WHO ASKED WHY

WRITTEN BY **Sowmya Rajendran**   ILLUSTRATED BY **Satwik Gade**

THWACK!

The stumps went flying!

Palwankar Baloo had won the match for his team. They rushed towards him to celebrate. He was their hero.

Baloo was Bhim's hero too. Like Bhim, he was an Untouchable. Until just a few years ago, Baloo's team wouldn't even eat with him. But this didn't stop him from becoming a great cricketer.

As a child, Bhim knew that the world he lived in was like a ladder. Different groups of people made the different steps of the ladder. Bhim knew that he belonged to the lowest step.

People above his group on the ladder did not eat with them. They did not drink water from the same well as them, or bathe in the same pond. They did not pray in the same temples.

They said people like Bhim could not even be touched.

As he grew up, Bhim began to understand that these groups were called castes – that there were high castes and low castes.

Bhim was a Mahar. He belonged to a low caste.

An Untouchable caste.

Even when he was little, Bhim had big ideas.

He wanted to study. He wanted to read books.

When can I go to school? he pestered his parents.

His father, Ramji, sighed. He was an officer in the army under the British who ruled India, and had managed to send all his children to school. Bhim was the last of his fourteen children.

Bhim's mother, Bhimabai, knew why her husband was sad. She was too. They both knew how he would be treated in school.

At the age of five, Bhim went to school just like his brothers and sisters before him. And like them, he could not sit with the rest of his class. He had to sit in a corner with a few others like him, the Untouchables.

Bhim knew the rules already. He had to sit on an uncomfortable gunny sack that he brought from home. He couldn't touch anything in the school.

WHY?

The teachers wouldn't touch his slate.

If he wanted water, the school assistant would pour it down into his hands, so that even the water pot didn't touch him. If the assistant didn't come to school, he and other Untouchable children like him would have no water to drink the whole day.

But none of this stopped Bhim from going to school.

There was one teacher, Mahadev Ambedkar, who was very fond of Bhim. He belonged to a high caste, at the top of the ladder.

He shared his lunch with Bhim sometimes. He even changed Bhim's last name to his own in the school records. So from then on Bhimrao Ambavadekar became Bhimrao Ambedkar.

One summer when he was nine years old, Bhim, his brother and cousins were going to visit his father in Koregaon. Just the four children, alone by train! Bhim was very excited.

Ramji, Bhim's father, had told them to get off the train at Masur. He would send someone to pick them up. But when the children reached the station, there was nobody waiting for them. Ramji had not received their letter telling him when they'd arrive.

The station-master came up to them, smiling. Such nice children, he thought. So well dressed. So polite. You must be high caste children, he told them.

No, said Bhim, we are Mahars.

The station-master's smile disappeared.

Untouchable children! He wanted nothing to do with them.

Finally, the children set off for Koregaon in a cart. The cart-driver wouldn't drive the cart sitting with them. He walked alongside and the children drove the cart themselves.

It was a long ride. By night, the children were tired and very, very thirsty. But nobody gave them water or shelter – not to Untouchables. By the time they reached Koregaon, all the joy of the trip was gone. They were exhausted, hungry, tired and sad.

Bhim never forgot that journey.

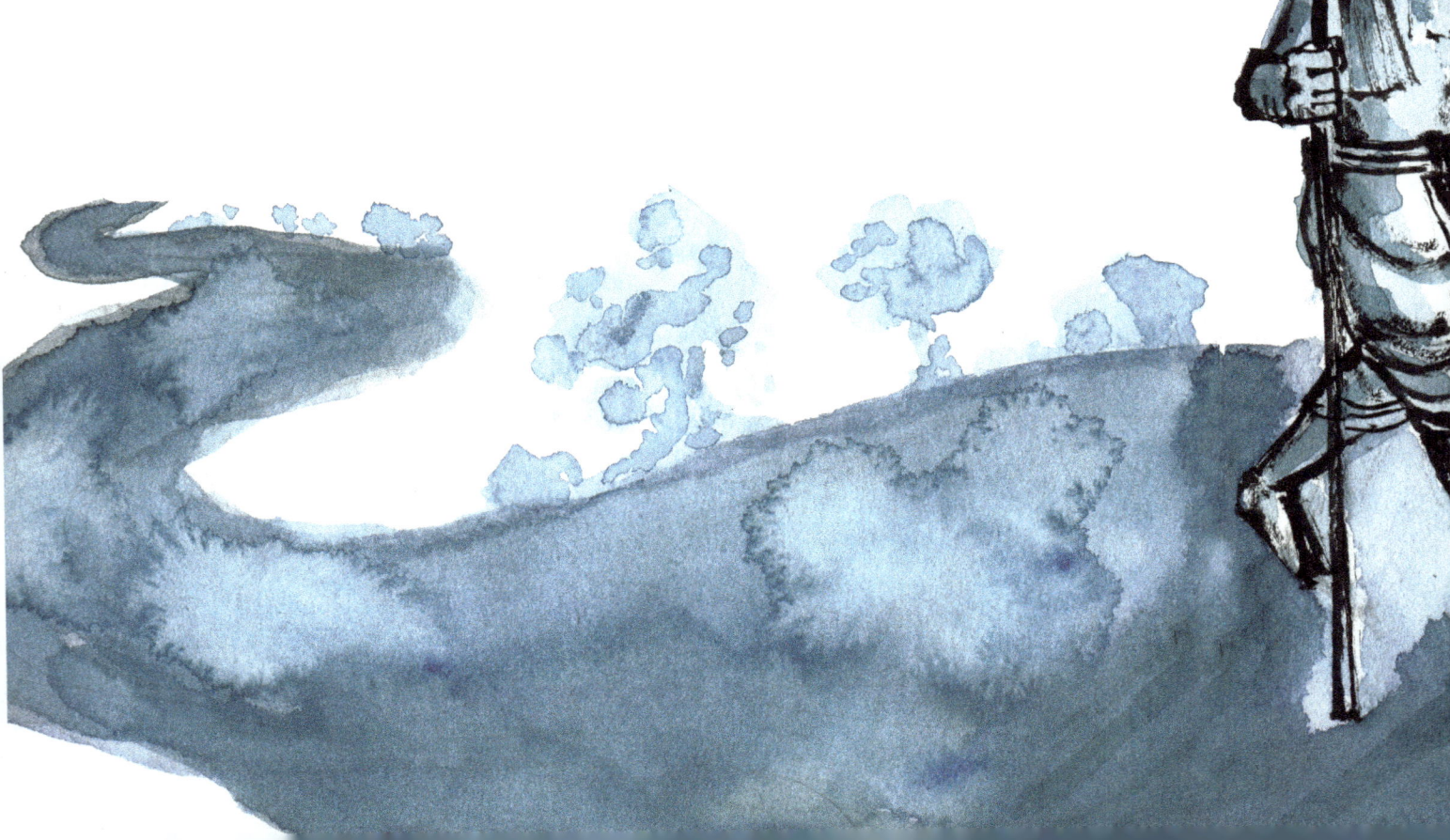

When Ramji moved with his family from their village in Maharashtra to Bombay, he put Bhim in one of the best schools in the city. All of them lived in one room on a crowded, noisy street. Bhim's father would wake him up at two in the morning every day – so that he could do his homework and study when everything was quiet!

Even in the big city, Bhim was treated as an Untouchable.

After school, Bhim went to college. He did so well that he won a scholarship to study in America.

There he discovered that he could go where he wanted, sit anywhere, drink and eat from the same cups and plates as others around him. For the first time, no one thought he was an Untouchable.

Bhim came back to India. At his first job, the assistants in the office threw files and papers at him because they didn't want to touch him.

Nobody would take orders from him because he was an Untouchable. He even struggled to find a place to live.

WHY?

Later, Bhim began to teach in a college. Even though he was a brilliant teacher and the students loved him, the other teachers refused to share their jug of water with him.

Bhim was not silent. He started a weekly magazine in which he wrote about caste and its evils.

In his country everyone was not equal.

The British who ruled India looked down upon Indians. And Indians looked down upon other Indians too! Many years had passed since the station-master had walked away from the young boy, but not much had changed.

Bhim was now highly educated. But that didn't make a difference to those who only looked at him as an Untouchable.

He was determined to do something about this. So he went to London to study law. It would help him bring justice to his people.

When he came back, Bhim continued his fight. In his speeches and writings he demanded equality for all castes.

He now had thousands of followers, who called him Babasaheb with affection.

One day, Babasaheb led a peaceful march to the public tank in Mahad near Bombay, from which Untouchable people had never been allowed to take water. He knelt down and drank water from it.

Thousands followed his example and broke a rule that had been in place for hundreds of years.

By now, Babasaheb was respected as a brilliant lawyer. He was the first person from his community to hold a PhD degree. When India became independent in 1947, he became the first Law Minister. Along with other experts, he wrote the laws of the land.

And so, the boy who was forced to sit in a corner of his classroom, picked up his pen to change the lives of millions in his country.

The laws he helped frame, make the Constitution of India.

Babasaheb believed that through law, he could give everyone in India – including the millions like him who were looked down upon as Untouchables – an equal chance in life. To eat and play, to study and work.

It is a fight that continues even today.

TIMELINE OF AMBEDKAR'S LIFE

1891 — Bhimrao Ramji Ambedkar was born in Mhow, India. The British ruled India at this time.

1901 — Ambedkar experienced the harrowing train and horse carriage ride described in the book, which left a lasting impression on him.

1908 — At age 16, Ambedkar entered Elphinstone College in Mumbai (then Bombay), becoming the first from his caste to ever do so.

1913 — Ambedkar came to the United States for the first time to study on a scholarship, and was intrigued by the equality he experienced in the US, even in those days.

1919 — Ambedkar advocated the creation of separate electorates for Dalits to ensure that they were adequately represented.

1927 — Ambedkar launched active movements against untouchability. He began with public movements and marches to open up public drinking water resources like those described in the story. They pre-date the Dandi March by Mahatma Gandhi.

1932 — Ambedkar successfully got seats reserved for Dalits within the general electorate. Due to his efforts, they obtained 148 seats in the legislature, instead of the 71 they would have otherwise received.

1947 — India became independent from British rule. Ambedkar was appointed as the nation's first Law Minister and Chairman of the Constitution Drafting Committee.

1949	The Constitution of India was adopted by the Constituent Assembly. It guaranteed and protected a wide range of civil liberties for individual citizens, including freedom of religion, the abolition of untouchability, and the outlawing of all forms of discrimination. Ambedkar also introduced a system of reservations of jobs in the civil services, schools, and colleges for members of under-represented minorities, a system akin to affirmative action.
1956	Ambedkar died in his sleep.
1990	The Bharat Ratna, India's highest civilian award, was conferred on Ambedkar posthumously.

GLOSSARY

Caste:
Hindu society was divided into broad groups in this order – Brahmins (priests), Kshatriyas (warriors), Vaishyas (traders), Shudras (laborers), and Dalits (earlier called Untouchables). Each group consists of numerous subdivisions. There have been many explanations for why society was ordered this way but one doesn't know for sure how caste came into existence or when it became a rigid system. Today, practicing untouchability is illegal, and most people who come from formerly Untouchable communities are called Dalits.

Gunny sack:
Similar to a burlap sack, it is made of jute or other natural fibers and is often used to store grains.

Slate:
A small chalk board used by students in school.

Stumps:
Wickets that are used in cricket, a sport played in many countries and very popular in India.

ADDITIONAL RESOURCES

Suggested Books:

Waiting For A Visa by Bhimrao Ambedkar (1935-36)

The Annihilation of Caste by Bhimrao Ambedkar (1936)

Puffin Lives: B. R. Ambedkar (2014, Chapter Book, also available on KitaabWorld.com)

Ambedkar: The Fight for Justice (2013, Graphic Novel, also available on KitaabWorld.com)

Websites:

For more information on Dr Ambedkar's life, speeches and writings:
http://drambedkarwritings.gov.in/content/

For a detailed timeline and information of his work:
http://www.columbia.edu/itc/mealac/pritchett/00ambedkar/

SOWMYA RAJENDRAN has written several books for children, from picture books to young adult fiction. Like many Indian children, Sowmya grew up reading about the country's freedom struggle but did not know much about Ambedkar and his inspiring life until much later. Although a very important personality in the movement, the uncomfortable questions that Ambedkar raised do not figure in most literature written for children. This picture book is an effort to share his story with children of this generation.

SATWIK GADE is an artist and designer with a special interest in illustration and typography. He enjoys reading books and is inspired by Indian mythology, comics, and Impressionist art. Illustrating children's books is his biggest fear and he is enjoying facing it!

PUBLISHED BY

At KitaabWorld, we advocate for awareness about South Asian culture through children's literature. We run a curated online bookstore for multicultural children's books, and conduct storytimes and teacher trainings on issues of diversity and representation.

Visit www.KitaabWorld.com for more information, including a teachers' guide for this book.

CPSIA information can be obtained
at www.ICGtesting.com
Printed in the USA
LVHW070140190820
663577LV00005B/146